WHERE I LIVE

Arundhathi Subramaniam is an award-winning poet and writer on spirituality and culture. Winner of the inaugural Khushwant Singh Memorial Prize for Poetry in 2015, the Raza Award for Poetry and the International Piero Bigongiari Prize, she divides her time between India and New York. She has published two books of poetry in Britain with Bloodaxe, *Where I Live: New & Selected Poems* (2009), which combines selections from her first two Indian collections, *On Cleaning Bookshelves* and *Where I Live*, with new work, and *When God Is a Traveller* (2014), a Poetry Book Society Choice which was shortlisted for the T.S. Eliot Prize, won the inaugural Khushwant Singh Prize at the Jaipur Literary Festival, and was awarded the International Piero Bigongiari Prize in Italy. Her latest collection, *Love Without a Story*, is published by Bloodaxe in 2020.

She has also written *The Book of Buddha* (Penguin, 2005) and *Sadhguru: More Than a Life* (Penguin, 2010), co-edited *Confronting Love* (Penguin, 2005), an anthology of Indian love poems in English, and edited *Pilgrim's India: An Anthology* (Penguin, 2011) and *Eating God: A Book of Bhakti Poetry* (2014).

Arundhathi Subramaniam

WHERE I LIVE

NEW & SELECTED POEMS

BLOODAXE BOOKS

ISBN: 978 1 85224 824 6

First published 2009 by
Bloodaxe Books Ltd,
Eastburn,
South Park,
Hexham,
Northumberland NE46 1BS.

www.bloodaxebooks.com
For further information about Bloodaxe titles
please visit our website and join our mailing list
or write to the above address for a catalogue.

Supported using public funding by
**ARTS COUNCIL
ENGLAND**

Cover design: Neil Astley & Pamela Robertson-Pearce.

Digital reprint by Lightning Source.

CONTENTS

DEEPER IN TRANSIT

ACKNOWLEDGEMENTS

The poems in the first two sections are reprinted from Arundhathi Subramaniam's collections *On Cleaning Bookshelves* (2001) and *Where I Live* (2005), both published in India by Allied Publishers.

The poems of *Deeper in Transit* are previously uncollected, and acknowledgements are due to the editors of the following publications in which some of these poems first appeared: *Carapace* and the *Poetry International Web*. Some of the poems are due to appear in the following publications: *Atlas*, SPARROW Women's Writing Anthology (2009), *tall-lighthouse* poetry anthology (2009) and *The Literary Review*.

ON CLEANING BOOKSHELVES

Blank Page

I am, for just this moment,
conquistador of the blank page,
my words stabbing
the white autocracy of silence,
as I survey the terrain,
contours, ravines, craters,
of an uncertain empire –
the splash of calligraphy,
the smudge of syllable
on unmapped paper.

And you who look away
as I seize this moment
and ride it fleetingly,
do you fear that if you look me in the eye
at this terrifying instant
of omnipotence,
that I shall surge
into your frontiers
and claim for my own
the sleeping mohenjodaros of your mind?

Heirloom

My grandmother,
wise even at eight,
hid under her bed
when her first suitor came home.

Grave and serene
her features, defined
as majestically as a head
on an old coin, I realise
through photographs, clouded
by the silt of seasons, like the patina
of age on Kanjeevaram silks,
that in her day, girls of eight didn't
have broken teeth or grazed elbows.

Now in her kitchen,
she quietly stirs ancestral
aromas of warm coconut lullabies,
her voice tracing the familiar
mosaic of family fables, chipped
by repetition.

And yet,
in the languorous swirl
of sari, she carries the secret
of a world where nayikas still walk
with the liquid tread of those
who know their bodies as well
as they know their minds, still glide
down deserted streets – to meet
dark forbidden paramours whose eyes
smoulder like lanterns in winter –
and return before sunset, the flowers
in their hair radiating the perfume
of an unrecorded language of romance.

The secret of a world
that she refuses to bequeath
with her recipes
and her genes.

The Archivist

Beloveds are best documented
out of the corner of the eye
where the retina bleeds
into the imagination.

You have the freedom now to archive
all that the taxonomists haven't yet sharpened
into points, cleaved into zones –
the austere collage of seasons
that is his face,
and the caesura of the navel
counterpointing the serrated comma
of a forgotten appendix operation.

Breathe deep
the wild marsh scent of groin,
wonder at the obstinate gradient
of toe and middle finger,
observe in the curve of calf
and flank, the karmic imprint
of a life that once lolled negligently
on pillows of silk and goose-feather.

Recognise too
the puzzled snarl
of pain that suddenly
winters the eyes.

Perhaps it would be wise now
to tell him of your love.
Profundities are best uttered in profile.

Sari

Worn soft with history
and hard water,
a sari in a field,
nine yards of womanslough,
issues soundlessly
into estuaries, archipelagos,
indentations, thrusts –
breasts
or buboes?
Snakeskin, wordless,
spinning out its own yarn,
with barley and sunshine,
of a rented body,
a life on lease.

5.46, Andheri Local

In the women's compartment
of a Bombay local
we search
for no personal epiphanies.
Like metal licked by relentless acetylene
we are welded –
dreams, disasters,
germs, destinies,
flesh and organza,
odours and ovaries.
A thousand-limbed
million-tongued, multi-spoused
Kali on wheels.

When I descend
I could choose
to dice carrots
or a lover.
I postpone the latter.

Madras, November, 1995

Secret garden, swimming
in the amniotic light of a green afternoon,
where the trees are familiar, the pink musanda,
the thunder's north-eastern baritone and its subtexts,
where much lies buried beneath generations of soil
and the thick sugarcane slush of rain –

a cosmic despair over algebra homework
rising with the aroma of turmeric and damp jasmine,

the silent horror of my grandmother
who watched her husband drive away her cats
through the stern geometry of her kitchen window,

my fourteen-year-old indignations
near dusty bougainvillea tresses
at belonging to a tribe of burnished brahmins
that still likes to believe its skin is curdled vanilla,

and the long amorous wail
of confectioned Tamil film songs
from the transistor of a neighbour's gardener, long dead.

No, I am not sentimental
about the erasure of dynastic memories,
the collapse of ancestral houses,
but it will be difficult to forget
palm leaves in the winter storm,
ribbed, fossilised,
against heaving November skies,
building up their annual heritage of anguish
before the monsoons end.

You and Marmalade

You and marmalade
help balance
the blood
of the daily newspaper.

But somewhere,
perhaps I forgot
what marmalade
and headlines
could do
to balance
you.

And so you grew
bloated, solar,
monstrous, before I realised
I had forgotten
other things as well –
my mother's voice
filtered through the crust
of morning dreams, leafy
and lozenge-cool,

and the warmth
of an unpolished
vitaminised grain
of a poem, just born.

One day, my love,
I will be fair to you.
I'll cut you down to size.

Madurai

Madurai,
land of Kannagi and Kovalan,
yours is a legendary tryst with fire.
Yet all I remember of you
is the fresh stain of sunlight
in some forgotten portico at the temple
of the fish-eyed goddess. I did wonder
briefly then at she who remains
unmoved by the fire
of daily ritual, by the damp swarms
of devotees, their bodies tattooed
by rivers of perspiration, surging ahead
to slake their thirst in her jewelled
marine gaze.

Madurai,
I realised your lineage could be mine
when I met Punditji.
Punditji who denounced me as modern
for not wanting to bear a child, for not wanting
my husband's name to be my own.
Punditji with a face about as medieval
as nylon, non-crushable,
drip-dry, not a crevice of doubt
in its pink florality.
Punditji who did not know, as I did not
till now, that I am descended
from an ancient tribe of women
capable of damning entire Madurais
to eternal infernos
with a sorcery
born not of virtue,
but of rage.

Amnesia

(Bombay, January 1993)

In your arms,
an entire metropolis
of memory
sinks out of sight.
Here are no purple epilepsies
of earth, no charred biographies,
no well-foddered certainties bloating
in cold rigor mortis,
no flesh curdling
under a January sun.
Not here.
Not yet.

In your mouth
of dew and cinnamon and starlight,
blind antennae create
their own flickering lexicons,
and I taste the fern-cool transience
of a lagoon of language,
without sediment.

Niagara

Bilious
with the candy and cellophane
of tourist safaris,
I approach Niagara,
prepared to be immune
to the pyrotechnics of surf,
the buttery foam and bluster
of first-world hydraulics,
the soap-operatic patterns
behind natural laws,
the metronomic drone
of some jaded cosmic box-office.

So why in the softer mud
of tactile memory
does the spray leave
such a laceration?
An eternal performance
of water paralysed
in a torrent of rage,
the hysteria, guttural,
venomous, of some tireless glottis
of the earth.

And why,
when I return,
am I
afraid?

On Manori Beach

That night we were sure
we were meant to be larger than this –
our days chewed to ragged edges
by invisible silverfish of doubt,
the wilderness of our interiors
whittled down to embattled networks
of trachea and lung.

Surely we were meant
for greater volume,
more picaresque mobility –
to ease our expanse
into the coves and inlets of this harbour,
to transact freely
with air frosted with salt,
to trace the distant contours
of promontories with our gazes,
yes, and even leave
our footprints on the sand.

At what point did we forget
that we could be actors
in this daily extravaganza
of space?

Moment of Ivory

(to Jane Austen)

Your world
where relations are a matter of social algebra
comforts me now.

Is it the distance between us that renders picturesque
the gowns of apricot taffeta,
the hot corseted moralities,
the ruthless certitudes of genteel parlours?

Or is it your heroines?
Their minds dark and cellar-chilled,
their conversations succinct as lace handkerchiefs,
even their rages citric,
never trailing threads of mottled passion
out of the interstices of their lives,
their composure echoed
in the dulcet symmetries of crochet,
the measured tread of moorland walks,
the equipoise of reading books by open windows,
unperturbed by the melancholy
of dusk landscapes.

Bless us, Jane,
my lover and I,
with lime-green shards
of crisp ironic wit
and the secret gift of tenderness
without the deceptions of caramel.

Sister

Supple as wisteria
her plait of hair across our beds –
my talisman at the age of five
against torch-eyed gods and ancestors
who leaked nocturnally
out of cupboards, keyholes,
the crevices of festering karmas.

Later
we drank deep draughts
of monsoon wind together,
locked eyes in mistrust,
littered our bedroom with books, fuzzy battle-lines,
quivering dominions of love and malice,
even as we ruptured time,
scooping world upon world
out of cavernous weekend afternoons
through the alchemy of mutual dream –
turquoise summers over ruined Mycenae,
the moon-watered stone of Egyptian temples,
and those times we set the zephyr whispering
under the black skies of Khorasan.

Clothes were never shared,
diaries zealously guarded,
but in the hour before the mind
carves out its own fiefdoms of memory,
we dipped into the same dark estuaries
of lust, grief and silted longing.

Now in rooms
deodorised into neutrality,
we sniff covertly
for new secrets, new battles, new men,
always careful to evade

the sharp salinity of recollection,
anything that could plunge us back
to the roiling green swamp of our beginnings.

But tonight if I stood at my window
it would take very little
to swing myself across
to that blazing pageant of peonies
that is your Brooklyn back-garden,
careening across continents
on that long-vanished plait of hair,
sleek with moonshine,
fragrant with Atlantic breezes.

Cardiac Care Unit

In this room
where the tube-light casts no shadows
and the illumination is disinfected.

Where the walls are the virulent blue
of neonatal Krishnas who cavort
through calendars, flabby on milk and adoration.

Where the painting
of the corpulent red rose
amid a fuzz of briars silkily
proclaims its botanical blessing –

May everyday
            be beautiful
                        to you.

(And all the time
the white plastic curtains flap
to their own
inscrutable biorhythms,
smugly eternal.)

In this room
where no malefic winds
are permitted to enter.
In this room
that transcends all seasons.
In this room
that withholds
the freedom to die,
kitsch has its own powers of healing.

Who Caught and Sang the Sun in Flight
(for Kartik)

You spoke with conviction
of the terrorism of the state.
And I, hesitant,
of those fraught landscapes of the mind.

The vodka clouded sentimentally,
a cordial of fuzzy peace,
making us believe, almost,
in a shared folklore,
a common heritage of warriorship.

That traditional repertoire of ripostes,
slippery pink with undergrad wisdom,
some kisses, moon-chilled, inevitable,
in a darkened car,
photographs, mirth-riddled,
fast fading into a generic sepia,
and cups of tea, burnt orange
by the rage and sunlight of college cafeterias.

But on nights of black slate,
buses, old insomniacs,
have long had the habit
of erasing pedestrians,
sometimes friends.
Like you, they rarely equivocate
in matters of life
or death.

And so, comrade with an alien vocabulary,
seeker on a journey I almost understood
in a sly, crustacean sort of way,
one night you flattened

in an instant
from rebel,

splendid, young,
tormented,
to reminiscence.

And the vodka doesn't taste of sunshine anymore.

To the One Who Dreams

(for Felli)

To the one who dreams she is the pin-up idol
of the great leopards that roam
the mountains of Tibet and Nepal.

To the pink resoluteness of her nose
and the seductive histrionics of her tail.

To the cabbalahs sealed in her frosted eyes
and her unerring awareness of where she begins and ends.

To her limbs swathed in a chiffon of languor
and her body tensile with the jungle wisdom
of a primeval huntress.

My bonsai lioness,
my storm-in-a-teacup,
my empress of the atomic ego,
to your faith
that a languid wave of imperial paw
is enough to reinvent
an inimical cosmos.

Sewage Psalm

(for my mother)

I've never quite understood
your plumbing –
what rumbling cistern feeds
your self-containment;
what tortuous whorl of drains
siphons off the blood
that must surely rise, restless,
behind your closed lids at night;
how you tame those torrents
of pounding anarchy
into ebb-tides that swim,
muddy-imaged,
in your eyes.

And it remains a mystery to me,
how you allowed a fragile bubble
of treacherous technicolor hope
to explode
into the flaming hullabaloo
of yet another life,
deciding terrifyingly
to forego
the option to despair.

On Cleaning Bookshelves

Begin by respecting the logic
that governed earlier conjunctions –

respect the hauteur
of the book not journeyed,

the complicit camouflage
of the borrowed paperback,

the frowning grandeur of the Russian classics,
upper shelf, upper caste,
lost in the austerities of a glacial tapas,

the sly tight-lipped smile
of the coffee-table volume,
lusciously swathed,
venerable geisha,

and the amber geniality
of the leatherbound coterie,
still fragrant with the smoke
of old cheroots
from colonial living rooms.

Then trace the occult insignia of silverfish
on paper that crumbles at a touch
into dragonfly-wingdust.
Rediscover the flyleaf inscription
of a lover's ex-lover,
damply intimate,

> and rising somewhere
> the crushed
> azalea scent
> of Manderley...

Tumbling unexpectedly
out of the mists of mothball
and nostalgia, a world
of lighthouses off the Devonshire coast
and dungeons stuffed with precious ingots –
embrace the lost world of Enid Blyton,
blessed Blyton,
beloved reactionary.

Now comes the chance to intervene,
match-make, infiltrate –
allow Kerouac
to nudge familiarly
at Milton,
Mira at Shankara,
watch Nietzsche sniff suspiciously
at Krishnamurti.
And listen close,
as Ghalib in the back row
murmurs drowsily
to Keats.

Open trunks.
Allow the musk
of a buried adolescence to surface
as Kahlil Gibran and Swinburne return
to claim their share of daylight and liberty
with all the dust
and truculence
of the unjustly exiled.

And amid the whispers
of reunion and discovery,
the hum of interrupted conversations
resumed after centuries,
know that it is time
to turn away.
And accept finiteness.
Accept exclusion.

Blaze On

And love too shall cool,
the sun hardening its viscosity
and lunar indifference quieting
its jagged belligerence
into peace
and crystals –
austere and brilliant
with trapped sunlight
and unforgotten energies, luminous
with the countless reflections
of past lives
of rich liquid ardour.

Until then,
my love,
let us blaze on.

I Am Impressed

I can hear the well-greased throb
of your chromium motorcycle mind
bullworked into maleness
revving into action
as you peel clichés like bananas.
I am impressed.

I can hear the menacing ripple,
the steely bulge
of your biceps
as you clinch your argument
with sleek after-shaved assurance.
I am impressed.

I can hear the pages
of yesterday's newspaper
flapping noisily, emptily,
between your legs.
I am
impressed.

Postcard from a Congealing Moment

This afternoon soaked
in a catatonia of sun
promises to last forever.

Tropical paradises have a way of knowing
that their business
is to remain imperturbable despite
the apoplexies heaving beyond
their postcard edges.

The birds, tracing
a slow raga of movement
against a coconut-milk sky,
are aware that their flight must end
where it began.
And the palm trees, filtering
solar vapours into glazed acres
of sand, never forget
that it is the rippling unison
of their spinal curvatures that holds
the entire picture in place.

Tropical afternoon,
we surrender once more
to your decree
of immutability.

Amoeba

You are linear
without bulges.
You are not me –
red, unformed, gelatinous –
in hidden crannies,
and even if you were,
I know I must not see it.

Not even if I dared
to be an amoeba.

No more
than a smudge of organic paste,
no skins of memory,
no faces swirling in my cytoplasm,
a single inviolable nucleus,
unselfconscious and yet aware
of my fluctuating frontiers,
never burgeoning with too many selves,
no messy nuclear explosions,
a simple solution to every cellular crisis –
sever self from self.

But would there be just a fleeting recollection,
just that familiar twinge,
as I watched you,
self-contained and immaculate,
swim like a virgin
into your unruffled watery domain?

At the Doors of Closed Rooms

I long for a poem
that will offer you
the enchanted balm of metaphor,
rather than slick polyester clichés
about women battered
by the men they love.
But it is difficult.

I want to tell you that I do know
of the guerrilla secrets of intimacy,
the lunacies that claw
at the doors of closed rooms,
that I am just as wary
of magisterial verdicts
because doubt remains for me
a matter of the gastric juices,
not some alkaline theory
of the mind.

And when you tell me your story is unique,
I believe you,
although others have said the same
of theirs. But neither shaman now,
nor poet, I offer you only the thin solace
of my rage and this one unwavering certainty –
no, I cannot believe love was ever meant to be like this.

Words

Words this evening are weapons.
We use them with easy precision
in shaft and counter-shaft,
our mutilations
Spielberg-swift, casual,
even artistic.

We who know
that the perfect line
that blinks up,
kitten-eyed, from the page,
is birthed
in the shiver of intestine
and visions malarial,
in the hiss
of detonating dream,
in the terrifying surrender
to absence.

We who know
that artisans must build
only to blast
vast ziggurats of thought
into silence.

We who know.
We who forget.

Back Soon

Some mornings
you know you've had enough
of standing sentry,
shutting windows, doors,
checking the bolt and safety-latch,
against the blind buffalo strength
of a world of consequence
running its own course.

You give up policing
fragile ecosystems
of hope and conversation and memory
against tectonic plates, shifting and grumbling
according to some primitive factory logic
of geology and vengeance.

Some mornings
you know you've had enough.
You wander into a dusty hinterland,
leaving gates open, outposts unmanned,
so when the world arrives, gurgling
in imperial anticipation,
or even when some capricious deity
comes a-knocking,
you're too far in,
too far gone
to care.

My god,
I've watched and waited,
listened and nodded,
murmured and clucked and smiled.

Now allow me
idiosyncrasy.

Winter, Delhi, 1997

My grandparents in January
on a garden swing
discuss old friends from Rangoon,
the parliamentary session, chrysanthemums,
an electricity bill.

In the shadows, I eavesdrop,
eighth grandchild, peripheral, half-forgotten,
enveloped carelessly
by the great winter shawl of their affection.

Our dissensions are ceremonial.
I growl obligingly
when he speaks of a Hindu nation,
he waves a dismissive hand
when I threaten romance with a Pakistani cricketer.

But there is more that connects us
than speech flavoured with the tartness of old curd
that links me fleetingly to her,
and a blurry outline of nose
that links me to him,
and there is more that connects us
than their daughter who birthed me.

I ask for no more.
Irreplaceable, I belong here
like I never will again,
my credentials never in question,
my tertiary nook in a gnarled family tree
non-negotiable.

And we both know
they will never need me
as much as I, them.
The inequality is comforting.

Vigil

As shadows lengthen,
as the horizon smudges
into secrecy,
as the ocean withdraws
into a misty November opacity,
feelings begin to grow more medieval.

And I long for you
as other lovers have before me
in a great melodic deluge
awash through history,
veined silver with melancholy,
deep-throated, brine-flecked, with yearning.

Twilight is the light
for lyric poetry,
a stab of blue kingfisher poetry,
a small blaze of longing
and regret
that is almost love,
too slight for immortality,
too intense to go unsung.

I almost understand now
why the women
in those poems I've ritually deplored.
wandered over to their mirrors,
tracing against their lips
the winestain of an unforgotten passion,
coiling against their necks
seething torrents of hair
into a muted tempest,
still electric with desire.

And it feels like I too could
wait for you,
while I perform
the erotic liturgies of another world,
wait for you,
who understands like none other
the prosody of my breath,
wait for you
and you alone.

But only until the light fades, my love,
only until the light fades.

By Thirty

By thirty
the midriff thickens
to remind you
of the babies you never brought to fruition.
Satori is a deferred project.

By thirty
you begin to smell death
on dawn visits to bathrooms.
You know it's a matter of waiting
until it's whirled away –
the whispers, creamy with love, aromatic
with the attar of last night's confidences
and the simple faith of early mornings.

By thirty
you accept that you'll never shop duty-free
at Reykjavik airport.
You postpone the course in film history
to another lifetime.
You begin to rediscover
an insular passion for melted jaggery.

By thirty
you can almost smile
at the treachery
of friends, lovers, schoolteachers.
Perhaps by forty
you'll forgive them.

By thirty,
you know you want to walk
away from ruined empires of fermented dream
towards lands vast and unchoreographed,
where every step ahead is adventure,
and every step ahead, anchorage.

Arunachala

(at the ashram of Ramana Maharishi, Tiruvannamalai)

I don't make sense of it yet
but it's all right for me to be here.
Here in this silence, dark as an old granary,
veined by the screech of peacocks,
and from the kitchen beyond,
the murmured cadences, tamarind-brown,
of a language I once blindly trusted.
And outside the window always
the opaque magic
                    of Arunachala –
the harsh grandeur
of grace, distilled
in rock and light and gaunt shadow.

It feels like given time
I could understand something here
about the eczemas
of grief and rage and grief,
about weekdays that must follow weekends,
the mintgreen underbelly
of grime-roughened thought.

It will come again,
the fear of the darkening flesh,
of watching the self turn to rind.

But for now this is enough.

For somewhere here, I know,
is something black,
something large,
something limpid,
something like home.

Prayer

May things stay the way they are
in the simplest place you know.

May the shuttered windows
keep the air as cool as bottled jasmine.
May you never forget to listen
to the crumpled whisper of sheets
that mould themselves to your sleeping form.
May the pillows always be silvered
with cat-down and the muted percussion
of a lover's breath.
May the murmur of the wall clock
continue to decree that your providence
run ten minutes slow.

May nothing be disturbed
in the simplest place you know
for it is here in the foetal hush
that blueprints dissolve
and poems begin,
and faith spreads like the hum of crickets,
faith in a time
when maps shall fade,
nostalgia cease
and the vigil end.

WHERE I LIVE

Where I Live

For a Poem, Still Unborn

Over tea we wonder why we write poetry.
Ten people read it, anyway.
Three are committed in advance
to disliking it.
Three feel a vague pang
but have leaking taps and traffic jams
to think about.
Two like it
and wouldn't mind telling you so,
but don't know how.
Another is busy preparing questions
about pat ironies
and identity politics.
The tenth is wondering
whether you wear contact lenses.

And we,
as soiled as anyone else
in a world addicted
to carbohydrates
and conversations without pauses,

still groping
among sunsets and line lengths
and slivers of hope

for a moment
unstained
by the wild contagion
of habit.

Where I Live

(for Anders who wants to know)

I live on a wedge of land
reclaimed from a tired ocean
somewhere at the edge of the universe.

Greetings from this city
of L'Oréal sunsets
and diesel afternoons,
deciduous with concrete,
botoxed with vanity.

City of septic magenta hair-clips,
of garrulous sewers and tight-lipped taps,
of '80s film tunes buzzing near the left temple,
of ranting TV soaps and monsoon melodramas.

City wracked by hope and bulimia.
City uncontained
by movie screen and epigram.
City condemned to unspool
in an eternal hysteria
of lurid nylon dream.

City where you can drop off
a swollen local
and never be noticed.
City where you're a part
of every imli-soaked bhelpuri.

City of the Mahalaxmi beggar
peering up through
a gorse-bush of splayed limbs.

City of dark alleys,
city of mistrust,
city of forsaken tube-lit rooms.

City that coats the lungs
stiffens the spine
chills the gut
with memory

City suspended between
flesh
     and mortar
          and faux leather
               and delirium

where it is perfectly historical
to be looking out
on a sooty handkerchief of ocean,
searching for God.

Madras

I was neither born nor bred here.

But I know this city

> of casuarina and tart mango slices,
> gritty with salt and chilli
> and the truant sands of the Marina,

the powdered grey jowls of film heroes,

> my mother's sari, hectic with moonlight,
> still crackling with the voltage
> of an M.D. Ramanathan concert,

the flickering spice route of tamarind and onion
from Mylapore homes on summer evenings,

the vast opera of the Bay of Bengal,
flambéed with sun,

and a language as intimate as the taste
of sarsaparilla pickle, the recipe lost,
the sour cadences as comforting
as home.

It's no use.
Cities ratify
their connections with you
when you're looking the other way,

annexing you
through summer holidays,
through osmotic memories
of your father's glib
lie to a kindergarten teacher
('My mother is the fair one'),

and the taste of coffee one day in Lucca
suddenly awakening an old prescription –
Peabury, Plantation A
and fifty grams of chicory
from the fragrant shop near the Kapaleeshwara temple.

City that creeps up on me
just when I'm about to affirm
world citizenship.

To the Welsh Critic Who Doesn't Find Me Identifiably Indian

You believe you know me,
wide-eyed Eng Lit type
from a sun-scalded colony,
reading my Keats – or is it yours –
while my country detonates
on your television screen.

You imagine you've cracked
my deepest fantasy –
oh, to be in an Edwardian vicarage,
living out my dharma
with every sip of dandelion tea
and dreams of the weekend jumble sale...

You may have a point.
I know nothing about silly mid-offs,
I stammer through my Tamil,
and I long for a nirvana
that is hermetic,
odour-free,
bottled in Switzerland,
money-back-guaranteed.

This business about language,
how much of it is mine,
how much yours,
how much from the mind,
how much from the gut,
how much is too little,
how much too much,
how much from the salon,
how much from the slum,
how I say verisimilitude,
how I say Brihadaranyaka,

how I say vaazhapazham –
it's all yours to measure,
the pathology of my breath,
the halitosis of gender,
my homogenised plosives
about as rustic
as a mouth-freshened global village.

Arbiter of identity,
remake me as you will.
Write me a new alphabet of danger,
a new patois to match
the Chola bronze of my skin.
Teach me how to come of age
in a literature you've bark-scratched
into scripture.
Smear my consonants
with cow-dung and turmeric and godhuli.
Pity me, sweating,
rancid, on the other side of the counter.
Stamp my papers,
lease me a new anxiety,
grant me a visa
to the country of my birth.
Teach me how to belong,
the way you do,
on every page of world history.

I Live on a Road

I live on a road,
a long magic road,
full of beautiful people.

The women cultivate long mocha legs
and the men sculpt their torsos
right down to the designer curlicue
of hair under each arm.
The lure is the same:
to confront self with self
in this ancient city of mirrors
that can bloat you
into a centrespread,
dismantle you
into eyes, hair, teeth, butt,
shrink you
into a commercial break,
explode you
into 70 mm immortality.

But life on this road is about waiting –
about austerities at the gym
and the beauty parlour,
about prayer outside the shrines
of red-eyed producers,
about PG digs waiting to balloon
into penthouses,
auto rickshaws into Ferraris,
mice into chauffeurs.

Blessed by an epidemic
of desperate hope,
at any moment,
my road
might beanstalk
to heaven.

Strategist

The trick to deal
with a body under siege
is to keep things moving,

to be juggler
at the moment
when all the balls are up in the air,
a whirling polka of asteroids and moons,

to be metrician of the innards,
calibrating the jostle
and squelch of commerce
in those places where blood
meets feeling.

Fear.
Chill in the joints,
primal rheumatism.

Envy.
The marrow igloos
into windowlessness.

Regret.
Time stops in the throat.
A piercing fishbone recollection
of the sea.

Rage.
Old friend.
Ambassador to the world
that I am.

The trick is not to noun
yourself into corners.
Water the plants.
Go for a walk.
Inhabit the verb.

Home

Give me a home
that isn't mine,
where I can slip in and out of rooms
without a trace,
never worrying
about the plumbing,
the colour of the curtains,
the cacophony of books by the bedside.

A home that I can wear lightly,
where the rooms aren't clogged
with yesterday's conversations,
where the self doesn't bloat
to fill in the crevices.

A home, like this body,
so alien when I try to belong,
so hospitable
when I decide I'm just visiting.

Another Home

An apartment in Scotland,
as neutral as they come,
the kitchen sink an egg-white skull,
scoured clean of the slimy debris
of biography.

No threats to my privacy:
the doorbell doesn't work
and the porter grumbles
about delivering letters to residents
with polysyllabic foreign names.

I sniff for familiar smells,
old dogmas in the fridge,
foibles under the carpet,
muted accents of desire in bed

and there is nothing here,
but robust functionality.

I live each moment
pretending I'm someone else,
deception following me
into the most intimate spaces.

I play Tic-Tac-Toe
on the kitchen tiles,
then press pen to paper
to hold myself down,
wondering if gravity still works
when other glues give up the ghost.

And I am perverse enough
to dream life elsewhere
was simpler –

a world where some of the barks
were scratched by me
and others by those I love
and love to hate.

And I wonder if I've forgotten
how to live
without someone I despise
ringing my doorbell,
blowing the whistle
showing me the road
I don't want to follow.

Take up my space,
occupy my land,
but for just a little while longer
leave me proprietor
of my messy subcontinent
of demons.

Stains

The world demands
that we be present
each time it reaches our names
on its roster.

It wants us
to be attentive
to the wisdom
of bank tellers.

It demands that we salute
the ones who know
the best bargains,
whose universe is no bigger
than their vocabulary,
who always look
like their passport photographs.

It reminds us that life stains
democratically –
blood and coffee and gravy and time,
chicken-pox and paradox.

It reminds us
that there are no silences
without accents,
no emptiness
without serration.

I'm as corroded by doubt
as you are by certainty.

We meet in rust.

No

I wake in the mornings
to find the city at my window,
a giant mouth
that's forgotten how to close.

The telephone rings,
each ring a reminder
that I have been detected,

that I am She
whose e-mails pile up unanswered,
whose checklists grow
tangled,
matted,
unchecked.

She who is never on the right platform.
She who turns away
from importunate hands at car windows.
She who smiles when she doesn't mean it.
She who didn't vote at three elections.

But what no one guesses
is that it is She who after sundown
stalks the dark alleys,
hungry to annihilate anyone
who seeks to tame her
with clammy malarial tentacles
of guilt.

And on full-moon nights
She even dares
to look the world
square in the face
and say
no.

Claim

Day dawns without debts, without doubts
PABLO NERUDA

Before doubt octobers
the mind into a clammy stupor,
before the tongue furs
into clichés, before opinions
turn gouty,
grant us the innocence
of birdcall, unburdened
by a heritage of birds who have called
before, and better.

Let there be heat on this page,
and bile, and let us be part
of the magic, oh god,
don't leave us out.

Doubt again
and again doubt,
and I think of how many days
we have let slip
because others' voices
were louder than our own.

No, we don't serve up
neat styrofoamed verse.
We sprawl, we lumber, we stain.
We love like everyone else,
with the thick odour of pathology.

We are ink and syrup
and virulent acid.
We are the midgets
who turn in three strides
into lords of the universe.

We are here to restore order,
to put the voices – of books, lovers,
teachers, customs officials –
in their places.

We are the upstarts,
ready finally to take up space,
demand time,
settle down on the page.

Tomorrow

(for 'The Catalogue', 2003, a multi-media exhibition by artist Vidya Kamat)

It begins in the body –
behind the drizzle of breath,
the habit of bone,
in the violet light where desires
surge like electrons,
perhaps in the womb.

Dark with rumour,
destiny veiled, secrets numberless,
a space rife
with rage
and promise.

There are toxins enough here
to burn a crater through this page.

Enough of the wounded Surpanakha
to slice off a few noses before sun-down.

Contempt enough
to dismiss those who aren't friends
as simply so much noise.

Humus enough,
clotted and churning,
to dream a thousand planets
of rain-forested thought.

Fuel enough
to erase them
into centuries of ash.

And beyond
in the distant horizon,
in a flickering interval,
you see it rising to meet you –
a carnival of sun
and blood

and stillness.

How to Disarm

Class Photograph

It's always the girl in the middle row
in school photographs of Class Two –
the one with two plaits, gaze as vacant

as a chorus, the one whose name
is on the tip of your tongue,

as you leaf through old albums
on weekend afternoons, a name that never quite
manages to emerge from that muddle

of almost and not quite, until
one day someone casually mentions
she died ten years ago,

and then the click
of revelation –

blue water-bottle,
school-bus regular,
monopoliser of seesaws,

Ami Modi, more vivid and centre-stage
in the mind's proscenium
than ever before,

and you believe the details
must mean something, add up
to some vital clue

and you almost know what,
but the knowledge remains poised
on the tip of the tongue,

awaiting another nudge,
another infinitesimal lurch

into the bigger picture.

Side-gate

How easy to slip out
between the bars of school's mildewed side-gate

in the middle of recess,
zigzagging between games of kho-kho

and steaming lunch-boxes,
squeezing out when everyone sees

but no one notices,
darting across the lane past the ENT hospital,

then down the broad sweep
of arterial road, pelting southward

towards a sea as Arabian as the spirit
where it is possible to become what one has always been –

snorting steed with cumulous mane
pounding into the tides

foaming galaxies of unbottled fiction
deferred coastlines

endless nights.

Imran Khan

I remember the time we crowded
into the Oberoi lounge
to meet Imran Khan –
a buoyant bevy of schoolgirls
with satchels and prefect badges,
still downy with chalk-dust.

We called him on the lobby phone
and were dazed when he answered
until we discovered it was just a floor manager
in cahoots with a shop owner
who told us he'd driven away minutes ago
in a green Mercedes, and was unlikely anyway
to be interested in sweaty Class Eight kids
with the smell of lunch on their breaths.

When we went home that night
something had already slunk into our hearts,
something clammy
like shame at our nerve,
our bumbling forgetfulness of the old lesson
that many are called,
but few chosen.

Habitat

I think I was nine
when I told Sonal, Gunjan, Devki and Shalini
on the school bus
that I didn't understand why we wore clothes
except as a matter of seasonal cover.

The observation was casual,
the result instantaneous:
they'd have crossed themselves
if they'd known how.
Something heaved, shifted
and reconfigured,
and in minutes,
I was excluded.

I made up, of course –
eliding,
distracting, hoping
no one would see the strain
in the smile, the effort
in the blood vessel,
of trying desperately to belong
to the ranks of the immaculately attired,
those who waft into cloth
like homing pigeons,
always mindful of self and occasion.

I've realised since
that I'm not alone,
that there are others
who spend their lives trying
to fit into clothes without
a wrinkle, a crease, a doubt,
hoping they'll never get caught
halfway between shedding

a Jurassic hide and looking
for a more muslin
habitat of skin,
a more limpid way of getting
to the gist of themselves.

Things

There are times
when form resists touch,
refuses to yield
to coercion or command –
an obstinate conspiracy
between self-perpetuating
coffee cups and the frantic
bushfire of books, laundry, Chinese restaurants,

and everywhere
the great Indian middle class
bloating steadily
on duty-free.

A rabid wilderness
of matter slurps
up absences, ransacks space,
an insurgent cardiogram
      serrating the skyline,
          eclipsing the moon.

This is the end of the world
you should have anticipated –

the unstoppable garrulity of things.

Night Shift

The oldest fears are the last to go
like the pre-dawn dread
of a process as impersonal
and tribal as birth
or dream

when someone masked and familiar –
the absence in the cupboard –
reappears for that ancient night-shift routine:

to pry something intimate
wet and still unprepared
from an aeon of self-assemblage

something that should have known
that entrails must always aspire
to be asphalt,

that the unambiguity of day
was never meant to be trusted –
its promise of mountain wind and blue summer sea.

Then the servile cringe,
the desperate bargains of the diehard trader,
squawk,
squiggle of nerve and gut,

erasure of struggle,

before the civilities
of sun
and cereal
and the imperceptible click of the cupboard door.

First Draft

It's just old fashioned, they say,
to use pen and paper for first drafts

but I still need
the early shiver of ink
in a white February wind –

the blue slope and curve
of letter
         bursting into stream,

the smudge of blind alley,
the retraced step, the groove
of old caravan routes, the slow thaw

of glacier, the chasm that cannot be forded
by image.

And I need reprieve, perhaps a whole season,
before I arrive at that first inevitable chill

when a page I dreamt piecemeal
in some many-voiced moon-shadowed thicket

flickers back at me
in Everyman's handwriting

filaments of smell and sight
cleanly amputated –
Times New Roman, font size fourteen.

Nocturne in January

As you sleep, I wonder at you
and how you grew
long before I knew you –
blind nub of desire striking
into tissue, ancestral grudge into bone,

a tangle of nerve
and lust and tenacity
growing through habit,
distraction and hectic
improvisation, into this entire
foliage of self.

How much fear do you carry with you,
I wonder, how much scar-tissue in the soul,
how long since you paused
at the creak of memory in the knee,
visited the distant suburb of your foot,
listened to the mandarin silences of the heart,
journeyed like every pilgrim must
to the cold place in the stomach
where we forget to love ourselves?

And I want to pray for you
in the furry way that animals know –

if warmth is proof of love
may my presence within you
remain forever tropical.

Gap

The eyes will always be older
than anything we say.

Words begin in clarity,
cuneiform in wet clay,
begin in an untolled
                 morning air of the mind.

But then the pulmonary interface –
tone sharpens without warning
vitrifies, betrays,

a sentence heaves into view,
deflected by leaden vapours to

                              some unknown destination,
and words hang heavy between us,

exhausted as tea-bags,
more sodden than cliché.

Until we find ourselves in a simpler world,
trust something older,
more intimate, inflected,

trust the cursive silence
of the eyes.

Return

After so long you will be here again
and I will have to relearn how it works –

this dreaming playhouse of possibilities
choreographed by another accent
of weight and limb,

clusters of clothes and paper morphed
into new jigsaws of habitation

and those startled collisions of memory
and reality at the sounds

of a running tap, a muffled yawn,
the clink and stumble of presence
in another room.

And then the nights
when, turning over on the side,
the arm reaches out

and finds,
with some ancient riverine instinct,
a familiar lost tributary
of self.

Decoded

What is it about an armful
of animal presence
that makes you feel you could decode
a language that has always seemed
a little garbled, the basics
just out of reach,
something they forgot to include
in the school primer?

Home is this circumference
of arm, this sneaky impress of nose
against neck, this repose of fur.

Peace, an abandoned memory
of talon, a widening ripple of sleep in the eye,
an unbidden snore.

And for the rest,
the dictionary.

Reading the Leaves

Nothing like the cool
morning sanity of leaf
to remind you
green is the colour
of borrowed time.

Give thanks
for the strumpet apparel
of rhododendron,
the rococo benediction
of fern,
the exquisite courtesy
of palm,
a single
bleached
octave
of
undefeated
intent
that never litters its wisdom
on unsuspecting heads.

And acknowledge always
the inevitable peepul,
old sentinel,
trusted witness,
for confirming yet again
that it's not about justice,

just weather,
just waiting.

Olive Ridley in Kolavipalam

Turtle wheezing down the beach,
flippers flailing valiantly,

knows what it's like
to be bullock cart on the autobahn,

dork on prom night,
every rasping breath the death rattle

of a species,
of an outmoded
way of being,

and between breaths, the gaze –
unblinking,
deathless.

Ahead
it beckons –

> a lurching habitat
> of oceantide and dream
> the promise of life
> without investment
> without dividend
> in a salt-spangled
> present continuous.

Until land beckons again.

Deliverance always
an element away.

Recycled

Driving through the Trossachs I see
the picture I drew as a five-year-old
in Bombay – a rectangle
with two square windows,
isosceles roof, smoking chimney,
and girl with yellow hair
standing in the driveway,
flanked by two flower pots.

And there is comfort in knowing
what we are so often told,
that fancy has wings
and dreams come true,
even if it takes years
for them to take root
in some corner
of a foreign land
that is forever India.

Tree

It takes a certain cussedness
to be a tree in this city,
a certain inflexible woodenness

to dig in your heels
and hold your own
amid lamp-posts sleek as mannequins
and buildings that hold sun and glass together
with more will-power than cement,

to continue that dated ritual,
re-issuing a tireless
maze of phalange and webbing,
perpetuating that third world profusion
of outstretched hand,
each with its blaze of finger
and more finger –
so many ways of tasting neon,
so many ways of latticing a wind,
so many ways of being ancillary to the self
without resenting it.

The Same Questions

Again and again the same questions, my love,
those that confront us
and vex nations,
or so they claim –

how to disarm
when we still hear
the rattle of sabre,
the hiss of tyre
from the time I rode my red cycle
all those summers ago
in my grandmother's back-garden
over darting currents of millipede,
watching them,
juicy, bulging, with purpose,
flatten in moments
into a few hectic streaks of slime,

how to disarm,
how to choose
mothwing over metal,
underbelly over claw,
how to reveal raw white nerve fibre
even while the drowsing mind still clutches
at carapace and fang,

how to believe
this gift of inner wrist
is going to make it just a little easier
for a whale to sing again in a distant ocean
or a grasshopper to dream
in some sunwarmed lull of savannah.

Another Way

Reverb

Something is being dismantled,
something that was clunky

like armour, passé like petticoats
in a new world,

and I hope it's something in the head,
some ageing manual learnt by rote,

some mechanical way of parsing
a life-sentence.

Interval

There are times
when the moving pen pauses

and the hand following the liturgy
of a familiar recipe, freezes

knowing that something new is trying to be born.

It belongs to no one,
it needs space to test

an expanse of pinion,

needs to be allowed that gasp
between borrowed wisdom
                              and actual flight.

Perhaps this is the moment
when Parashurama recognises Rama,
recognises the need for space

between tenancies,
form and reform,

so that some old mistakes can be made again
and some not.

Resolve

To read long and wetly
without carrying away more

than is necessary
for a squelch of recognition,

a ferment of crickets
in the backyard,

starbursts
for dark nights.

Living Alone

is about learning

to believe
things are as they appear,

that every day has no
ulterior motive,

that every flicker of air against neck
does not spell a spectral presence,

about learning not to ask for more
than those long afternoons

gliding through rooms
and rooms

of vacant mind,
recovered after years of subletting.

Where Lentils Sleep

It's about how the day rests
on slabs
angled precariously –
a fragile architecture
of meaning.

Which is why this matters
the moment we look across
at each other, intent
                    fractured, in the split second
before choice, before the shadow
of the next brick.

And this matters too,
the silence behind the door,
the hush of granaries,
spiked with cardamom and chilli,

the deep slumber of lentils
before the first tremulous shoot
of dream.

What Matters

I tell you it's about your quest
and your creativity
and your tuneless songs in the kitchen,
and your happiness, runny,
sunlit, as egg yolk.

But that's not all.
It's actually this –
the warm tautsoft springy irrepressible
materiality of you,

you who give new life each day
to the weightless phantoms in your wardrobe,
you who leave behind rumpled sheets,
slippers, the lingering isotherm
of your presence on my bed –

I respect your spirit
but if you were here right now
I'd get on with what really
matters.

Rib Enough

The reason I need to see you
glowering over a newspaper every morning,
your face dewy with teasmoke,
is because life without ritual
would be body without ribcage.

But let there be just enough rib
between the two of us
for a rumour of edge –
frugal hint of rampart and crag –

and an ever-widening commune
of breath.

Kinship

Fixer of my fuse,
creature of the dawn, my edison,
my epiphany, playful wizard
of the hundred-watt filament,
flash your beam here
into this musty silence
of Burma teak, pitted
with woodlice memories of pride
and struggle and the way things were.

Let's celebrate our kinship
under the street lamps
where sodium vapour
is thicker
than blood.
Introduce me
to the circus pleasures
of halogen,
the sluttish allure
of neon, sooty with commerce
and amnesia.
Drench me
with the illicit vices
of bastard amber.

And let us walk together
over moon-brindled fields,
opal mountains of sunwashed snow,

to those forgotten places
where words crouch
in an infinity of waiting,

before slowly turning over on their side,
lathered with starlight.

Been There

How long it takes to reach
a moment
that is not the past

and even when you're there
it's difficult to be sure.

There is always something familiar
in the turn of a line,
the bend of a road,
an angle of neck,

a timbre almost native
in a stranger's voice,

even an alien language
stubbled with memory.

How long it takes to reach
the present –
the moment before you remember
you've been here before.

Counter

We thought it meant going against the grain,
and of course it did,
but not with clenched teeth
and knotted sinew

but by listening just beneath the skin –
the urgent gurgle of current,
rife with frogspawn,
pushing rapidly
upstream.

Locality

He says he dreams
of a cottage marooned
in a moon-flecked ocean of paddy,
she of a solitude
defined by crickets and oil lamps,

and I know I often long
for some warm lair
in a craggy wilderness
suffused by the trust of animals,
monsooned in grace.

We promise ourselves we'll do it one day
disentangle ourselves
from a world that would have us believe
this is the only way to live –
to follow the frantic zeal of streets
that hurry us all the time towards
offers open only till stocks last.

We tell ourselves we'll do it,
move out to a place
where drifting across oceans,
limned with dawn,
through ever-widening shoals of stars,
is simply a way of being
intensely local.

Another Way

To swing yourself
from moment to moment,
to weave a clause
that leaves room
for reminiscence and surprise,
that breathes,
welcomes commas,
dips and soars
through air-pockets of vowel,
lingers over the granularity of consonant,
never racing to the full-stop,
content sometimes
with the question mark,
even if it's the oldest one in the book.

To stand
in the vast howling, rain-gouged
openness of a page,
asking the question
that has been asked before,
knowing the gale of a thousand libraries
will whip it into the dark.

To leave no footprints
in the warm alluvium,
no Dolby echoes
to reverberate through prayer halls,
no epitaphs,
no saffron flags.

This was also a way
of keeping the faith.

DEEPER IN TRANSIT

Refaced

(after Imtiaz Dharker's 'Canvas')

Do I want another face?
Sometimes I do.

A face no longer disfigured
by need. A face you can turn
inside out like a sock,
never knowing the difference
between surface and interior,
soft as old wool, implacable
as peace, the fibres accustomed
to concavity,
to disuse. Accustomed
to my absence.

Black Oestrus

I could lie against you,
mouth on forehead, limbs woven
into a knot too dense
for yearning, hearing the gossamer flurry
of your breath, the wild nearness
of your heartbeat, and it still won't be
close enough.

I could swallow you,
feel the slurry of you
against palate
                    — and throat,
ravish you
with the rip, snarl
and grind of canine
and molar, taste the ancestral grape
that mothered you, your purpleness
swirling down my gullet,
and it would be a kind
of knowing,

but you still wouldn't be
me enough.

I'm learning, love,
still learning
that there's more to desire
than this tribal shudder
in the loins.

But I'm not sure
I'm ready
for it yet —

that shock
in your daily kabuki
of shape and event.

Not yet.

Not yet
that shock
of vacancy.

Rutting

There was nothing simple about it
even then –

an eleven-year-old's hunger
for the wet perfection

of the Alhambra, the musky torsos
of football stars, ancient Egypt and Jacques Cousteau's

lurching empires of the sea, bazaars
in Mughal India, the sacred plunge

into a Cadbury's Five Star bar, Kanchenjanga, kisses bluer
than the Adriatic, honeystain of sunlight

on temple wall, a moon-lathered Parthenon, draught
of northern air in Scottish castles. The child god craving

to pop a universe
into one's mouth.

It's back again,
the lust
that is the deepest
I have known,

celebrated by paperback romances
in station bookstalls, by poets in the dungeons
of Toledo, by bards crooning foreverness
and gut-thump on FM radio
in Bombay traffic jams –

an undoing,
an unmaking,
raw
raw –

a monsoonal ferocity
of need.

And this is about pain too

realising
how much of the inside
is pure slush

the centre more wobbly
than marmalade,
more roiling
than suburban gutters in August rains.

And then later,
a long time later,
the quiet –

but for how long?

Is this what they call dum pukht,
a slow cunning Awadhi simmer
of hormone and nostalgia
and recycled need,
a deep churning
of juices
in the clay innards
of a sealed vessel,

plotting mutiny
one day
but not yet?

Leapfrog

Anyone who has sufficient language nurses ambitions of writing a scripture
SADHGURU JAGGI VASUDEV

Not scripture, no,
but grant me the gasp
of bridged synapse,
the lightning alignment
of marrow, mind and blood
that allows words
to spring

from the cusp of breathsong,
from a place radiant
with birdflight and rivergreen.

Not the certainty
of stone, but grant me
the quiet logic
of rain,
of love,
of the simple calendars of my childhood
of saints aureoled by overripe lemons.

Grant me the fierce tenderness
of watching
word slither into word,
into the miraculous algae
of language,
untamed by doubt
or gravity,

words careening,
diving,
        swarming, un-
forming, wilder
than snowstorms in Antarctica, wetter

than days in Cherrapunjee,
alighting on paper, only
for a moment,
tenuous, breathing,
amphibious,
before
leaping
to some place the voice
is still learning

to reach.

Not scripture,
but a tadpole among the stars,
unafraid to plunge
deeper
if it must –

only if it must –

into transit.

Demand

And on days like this
nothing else will do.

Nothing but that whisper
of breath against the ear.

Breath that's warm
like the sigh of palmyra trees
in Tirunelveli plantations.

Breath
that's crisp
like linen, rice-starched,
dhoop-soaked,
in a family cupboard.

Breath
to be trusted,

with a thread maybe
of something
your foremothers never knew,
or pretended not to –
the spice-mist
of hookah on winter nights
in Isfahan, or raw splatter
of Himalayan rain, or wine
baroque with the sun
of al-Andalus.

Breath
of outsider,
ancestor,
friend,

who leaves nothing more than this
signature of air
against skin,
reminding you
that there's nothing respectable
about family linen
when cupboard doors close,

reminding you
that this
this uncensored wilderness
of greed
is simply –
or not so simply –

body.

Fit

Not a hand-me-down
not ready-to-wear,
but tailormade, hand-woven
in a loom unknown,
with pockets dark and roomy
(the left deeper than the right?),
softer than the saris my grandmother
wore as a young girl in Bauktaw,
with the faintest rumour
of dorsal fin
and wrinkles
where I need them.

How did you happen?

Lover Tongue

Perhaps I will tire
of your grammar,

find myself yearning
for the rumble of verb or the soft
flesh of pure vowel
on those mornings when I stumble
over your landscape
of unforgiving nouns.

And it's possible I will whittle away
the very ribcage
in which I once sought sanctuary,

gnaw at the unbending sinew
of ancestral norm,
sulk,
turn sophomoric,
say fuck you,
say cope up,
just to disrupt
your family symmetries
your patrician DNA.

Maybe I will simply
want something more
one day
than your bequest of semicolons –
something more final,
more silent.

But even if I turn the page
before you do,
remember I am as
dog-eared,

soiled,
puzzled,
as you are,
and as much in love.

Wearing High Heels

It was those heels
that I wore
to the Class Eight jam session.

They left red weals on my feet
as I stumbled
across the dusty J.B. Petit school hall.

But that night
the weedy boys
from the school next door
turned into something else –
lithe warriors,
medieval, almost epic,
dark, deccan,
bodies supple as bowstrings,
gait honed by a wisdom as old
as Patanjali
(with just a frisson
of Travolta),

their conversations fluent
as streams that burble
by motionless sages
in forest hermitages,

their senses alert
to jungle breath
and portents of sky
and recondite shifts
of womanweather.

I have grown
too tall for heels.

The boys have grown
into bankers
and soft-bellied intellectuals.

But when lights dim
and city drawing-rooms
turn vertiginous,
I see them all over again,
dark, feral,
lean-haunched,
shadowy,
shape whittled down
to what really counts –

men.

The Other Side of Tablecloths

Miss Guzder's outrage was moral:
A girl like you – I never expected it – how could you?

Before her, the underside
of my tablecloth –
snarling green mayhem
of equatorial rainforest,
seething beneath
an upfront view
of convent-educated daffodils.

Miss Guzder, you'd disown me still.
I unseam easily,
turn green even when determined
to stay twig-dry and rootless,
and though I always long
to be elsewhere,
I've never come unstuck
without turning
into a moist tangle
of filament, each straggling
fibre alive
to a self-inflicted
green carnage.

But I learn,
I learn,

and might just grow one day
into the seamstress you'd be proud of:

I'll suture and snip,
lazy-daisy and butcher,
love and leave,
no strings attached.

Almost Shiva

It's here again,
sweeping through my life,

ripping apart jeans, books, kurtas, income tax returns,
wiping the grin
off the Bhairavnath mask
from the Thamel street shop.

Except this time
there will be no cut-and-paste,
no frantic attempt
to get the lines right,
check the silver, count the spoons.

There's terror in the air

but as earthenware crashes
and something like flesh
blackens on the griddle,
I feel it –

the solar plexus lurch,
the shiver of guilt,

a mothwing flutter of authorship

Sharecropping

I'm wearing my mother's sari,
her blood group,
her osteo-arthritic knee.

We've voted
for different men, same governments.

In dreams she plays
among trees of rubber and betel palm
outside a home in Myanmar
while I scamper down
dark service stairways
in Bombay buildings, sharp
with the smell of urine
and kesar agarbatti
smoking out of the breast pocket
of the seventh-floor madman.

She lusted after Dev Anand,
I after Imran Khan.
On television
both still sport
headfuls of black hair.

She treads nimbly
across language.
I vowel every now and then
into mouldering inertias.

I come undone
with muzak
or a compliment.
My mother's made
of sterner stuff.

Sowing the same dream
in a different self –
the cussed logic
we both know
behind aeons
of parenting.

We talk Buddhism,
Lata Mangeshkar, plot pedicures,
late into the night,

and she watches me
ancient peasant
canny harvester,
her eyes bright
with defeat
as I grow stealthily
into her body.

Here it is then –
the treachery
of middle age,
of love.

It gets no closer than this, Mum.

Osteoporosis

You comment on the gait
of women in this country,
those above fifty,
how they roll shiplike from side to side.

Osteoporosis,
I say with the wisdom of my thirties,
a generation without HRT,

and then venture
to try the truth:
Where I live
intent doesn't translate
into action
without bottlenecks
at every joint,
every junction,
every circuit,
every street.

Sideways isn't a strategy here.
It's how we live.

Catnap

This shoebox started out
a stiff-upper-lipped quadrilateral,
Upholder of Symmetry, Proportion, Principle,
sanctuary to an upright couple
of pedigree leather moccasins.

This week
shoebox learns
to sigh
de-
    cant,
contemplate

gravity.

Old idealist softens,
grows whiskers,
paw,
drowsing chin,
slumped tail,
Arctic eye.

Form is emptiness
Emptiness is form, Shariputra.

Shoebox abdicates
shape
and Gucci worship,

secedes from
nostalgia.

Pukka sahib
learns
to purr.

A Shoebox Reminisces

I renounced shape
a long time ago,

chose
bagginess,

endless
recess-
ivity,

but there are days
when the longing
returns

and I cannot abide
the sterile cynicism
of the Anti Couples Club,
the smug peddlers
of Uni-sole Advaita.

I know it means
the saga of
two old shoes
all over again,

their grubby leather unions,
tales of childhood,
prejudice, toe jam, politics,

laces in a perpetual snarl
of knots,

footprints,

footprints.

But some days
I'm idolater enough
to want it again:
that old charade,

otherness.

Epigrams for Life after Forty

Between the doorbell
and the death knell
is the tax exemption certificate.

There are fewer capital letters
than we supposed.

Other people's stories will do.
Sticky nougatine green-and-pink stories.
Other people's stories.

Untenanting is more difficult
than unbelonging.

The body? The same alignment
of flesh, bone, the scent of soap, yesterday's
headlines, a soupçon of opera.

But there are choices
other than cringing vassal state
and walled medieval town.

And there is a language
of aftermath,
a language of ocean and fluttering sail,
of fishing villages malabared
by palm, and dreams laced
with arrack and moonlight.

And it can even be
enough.

Learning to Say Yes

They matter,
the minor questions –
the smell of a new wardrobe,
the eternal bus ticket
in the bag's second compartment, the leer
of the late shift security guard.

Yes, Draupadi's sari is endless

and there's no way to tame
life's wild unstoppable
bureaucracy
but this:

Fill out the form. Do it in bloody triplicate. Enroll.

Watching the Steamrollers Arrive

Language begins
to peel away from you,
the skin stretched,
no longer lubricated
by faith
in renewal.

Names have started
their dissolve. Letters smudge,
the neon is erratic, leaving half
the words in serrated eclipse.

The dots have lost
their jauntiness, the dashes their
bravado,

and the little that holds
quivers, knows

that something behind
is being
disembowelled
by an ancient buffalo logic,
unhurried,
systematic.

The police sirens, the barking dogs, grow louder.

Flagbearers

We have you covered –
Breakdown, depression, genetics, authoritarian upbringing, neural
damage, suppression, hubris, sublimation, addiction, Marxism, Kaliyug,
planetary configurations –

Our eyes gleam
with the fervour of priests
on sacred riverbanks,
ancient domesticators
of mortality.

Even the gods inch closer
when we brand them
with our love,
our naming.

The second battle of Panipat, Samsung TV, Raja Raja Chola, Fakhruddin
Ali Ahmed, Hawkins Pressure Cooker, J. Krishnamurti, I see I see I

And we cling,
chew,
suck,
our mouths stained
with the green salad of language,

and we pound
and chew again,
our jaws grinding the cud
of a timeless latex wisdom,

because we believe
because we must

that words tame,
words stanch,
words embalm,

words know.

Forever Connected

Geishas of the inbox,
our neural pathways paved,
synapses bridged, arteries
fibre optic, heart chakras unclogged
by the Great Express Highway,
our ducts sweetened by after-mint
and Kenny G, the peepul
between us felled
to unclutter the view,
our roads widened, drainage overhauled, stray dogs exterminated.

The lines on our route are never busy.

The arrangements are in place.
Love will follow.

Confession

*To take a homeopathic approach to the soul is to deal with
the darkness in ways that are in tune with the dark.*
                    THOMAS MOORE

It's taken time
to realise
no one survives.
Not even the ordinary.

Time to own up then
to blue throat
and gall bladder extraordinaire,

to rages pristine,
guilt unsmeared
by mediocrity,

separation traumas
subcontinental
and griefs that dare
to be primordial.

Time to iron out
a face corrugated
by perennial hope,

time to shrug off
the harlotry
and admit
there's nothing hygienic
about this darkness –
no potted palms,
no elevator music.

I erupt from pillars,
half-lion half-woman.

The floor space index I demand
is nothing short
of epic.

I still wait sometimes
for a flicker of revelation
but for the most part
I'm unbribable.

When I open the coffee percolator
the roof flies off.

Swimming

It's because you become
foetus at the funfair –/
whirling, whooping
through a jungle
of chlorine and pickled
Mediterranean blue.

Because you realise
it's enough to be
a ferris wheel of armlegarmleg
motored by turtle brain.

Because for a moment
you could even be Him,
the Lord of Tillai,
birthing, juggling,
slaying universes
in an inspired mayhem
of limb and lust.

Because deep within your seashell heart
you hear it again,
the oceanic roar
that reminds you
that it's happening
right now.

Life is here.